ELON MUSK.
THE LITTLE BLACK BOOK

"MAY THE WISDOM OF THE GREATEST MINDS
BECOME YOURS."
S. C. HOLLISTER

RENEGADE PUBLISHING

ELON MUSK. THE LITTLE BLACK BOOK

Design Copyright © 2015 S.C. Hollister

Published by Renegade Publishing

California

To Elon Musk,
Thank you.

Contents

The Little Black Book used to be a means of getting in touch with people who could give you what you wanted; most notoriously known as a Booty Call book.

But, in this 21st century version of the Little Black Book, wisdom and knowledge are the key to opening doors.

The design of this book invites you to meditate on the wisdom within, have focused conversations, or protect your coffee table from condensation.

May the wisdom of some of the greatest, become yours.

Elon Musk.
The Little Black Book

Elon's Little Black Book

~

1. "Tip number one – Work super hard."

2. "Optimism, pessimism, fuck that; we're going to make it happen."

3. "I think that's the single best piece of advice; constantly think about how you could be doing things better, and keep questioning yourself."

4. "Failure is an option here. If things are not failing, you are not innovating enough."

5. "No, I don't ever give up. I'd have to be dead or completely incapacitated."

6. "Starting a company is like eating glass and staring into the abyss. If you feel like you're up for that, then start a company."

7. "I like to be involved in things that change the world."

8. "Patience is a virtue, and I'm learning patience. It's a tough lesson."

9. "If something is important enough, you should try, even if the probable outcome is failure."

10. "I don't create companies for the sake of creating companies but to get things done."

11. "If we're all in a ship together and there's some holes in the ship, and we're bailing water out, and we have a great design for a bucket, even if we're bailing out way better than everybody else, we should probably share the bucket design."

12. "I would like to die on Mars; just not on impact."

13. "Great companies are built on great products."

14. "Persistence is very important. You should not give up unless you are forced to give up."

15. "Burning oil, which is quite precious, is like taking furniture from your house and setting it on fire for the heat."

16. "I could either watch it happen, or be part of it."

17. "Starting and growing a business is as much about the innovation, drive, and determination of the people who do it, as it is about the product they sell."

18. "When thinking about starting a business, I think it's actually better to start in a trough and come to market in a peak, than the other way around."

19. "It's okay to have all your eggs in one basket, as long as you control what happens to that basket.

20. "Life is too short for long-term grudges."

21. "I think it is possible for ordinary people to choose to be extraordinary."

22. "Rockets are cool. There's no getting around it."

23. "We will not stop until every car on the road is electric."

24. "The first step is to establish that something is possible; then probability will occur."

25. "It is very important to actively seek out and listen very carefully to negative feedback."

26. "When you struggle with a problem, that is when you understand it."

27. "Last year was a year of great achievement, but honestly, it sucked... I didn't have that much fun."

28. "There's a tremendous bias against taking risks. Everyone is trying to optimize their ass-covering."

29. "You want to be extra rigorous about making the best possible thing you can.

30. "When Henry Ford made cheap, reliable cars, people said, 'Nah. What's wrong with a horse?' That was a huge bet he made, and it worked."

31. "Boil things down to their universal truths, and reason up from there."

32. "I have absolutely no idea how to play the violin."

33. "I don't spend my time pontificating about high-concept things; I spend my time solving engineering and manufacturing problems."

34. "Seek negative feedback."

35. "If you go back a few hundred years, what we take for granted today would seem like magic; being able to talk to people over long distances, to transmit images, flying, accessing vast amounts of data like an oracle. These are all things that would have been considered magic a few hundred years ago."

36. "Really, the only thing that makes sense is to strive for greater collective enlightenment."

37. "We have this handy fusion reactor in the sky called the sun; you don't have to do anything – it just works. It shows up every day."

38. "You'll be able to travel for free, forever, on pure sunlight."

39. "At the start of Tesla and SpaceX, I thought we would most likely fail, but it would be worth it to try."

40. "Yeah, well I think anyone who likes fast cars will love the Tesla. And it has fantastic handling by the way. I mean, this car will crush a Porsche on the track, just crush it. So, if you like fast cars, you'll love this car. And then oh, by the way, it happens to be electric and it's twice the efficiency of a Prius."

41. "I just give it everything I've got irrespective of what the circumstances may be. You just keep going and get it done."

42. "I think it matters if someone has a good heart."

43. "I'm inspired by a lot of historical figures."

44. "Given a choice, I'd rather stick a fork in my hand than write about my personal life."

45. "Great companies start because the founders want to change the world, not make a fast buck."

46. "I think it would be great to be born on Earth and to die on Mars."

47. "It's remarkable how many things you can explode. I'm lucky I still have all my fingers."

48. "You want to have a future where you're expecting things to be better, not one where you're expecting things to be worse."

49. "Our goal here is to fundamentally change the way the world uses energy."

50. "If there was a way that I could not eat so I could work more, I would not eat."

51. "Tesla was my hero... but he was no rocket scientist."

52. "We could definitely make a flying car. The hard part is how do you make a flying car that's super safe and quiet? Because if it's a howler, you're going to make people very unhappy."

53. "Brand is just a perception, and perception will match reality over time. Sometimes it will be ahead, other times it will be behind. But brand is simply a collective impression some have about a product."

54. "Some people don't like change, but you need to embrace change if the alternative is disaster."

55. "I think life on Earth must be about more than just solving problems... It's got to be something inspiring, even if it is vicarious."

56. "I usually describe myself as an engineer; that's basically what I've been doing since I was a kid."

57. "The rumors of the demise of the U.S. manufacturing industry are greatly exaggerated."

58. "An asteroid or a super volcano could certainly destroy us, but we also face risks the dinosaurs never saw: an engineered virus, nuclear war, inadvertent creation of a micro black hole, or some as-yet-unknown technology could spell the end of us."

59. "I wouldn't say I have lack of fear. In fact, I'd like my fear emotion to be less because it's very distracting and fries my nervous system."

60. "If you're trying to create a company, it's like baking a cake. You have to have all the ingredients in the right proportions."

61. "You could warm up Mars, overtime, with greenhouse gases."

62. "I really do encourage other manufacturers to bring electric cars to market. It's a good thing, and they need to bring it to market and keep iterating and improving and make better and better electric car, and that's what's going to result in humanity achieving a sustainable transport future. I wish it was growing faster than it is."

63. "The odds of me coming into the rocket business, not knowing anything about rockets, not having ever built anything, I mean, I would have to be insane if I thought the odds were in my favor."

64. "If you want to grow a giant redwood, you need to make sure the seeds are okay, nurture the sapling, and work out what might potentially stop it from growing all the way along. Anything that breaks it at any point stops that growth."

65. "My background educationally is physics and economics, and I grew up in sort of an engineering environment – my father is an electromechanical engineer. And so there were lots of engineer-y things around me."

66. "The problem is that for a lot of big companies, process becomes a substitute for thinking. You're encouraged to behave like a little gear in a complex machine. Frankly, it allows you to keep people who aren't that smart, who aren't that creative."

67. "The space shuttle was often used as an example of why you shouldn't even attempt to make something reusable. But one failed experiment does not invalidate the greater goal. If that was the case, we'd never have had the light bulb."

68. "It's hard to break into a network once it's formed."

69. "Physics is really figuring out how to discover new things that are counterintuitive, like quantum mechanics – it's really counterintuitive."

70. "If you get up in the morning and think the future is going to be better, it is a bright day. Otherwise it's not."

71. "Self-driving cars are a natural extension of active safety and obviously something we should do."

72. "I'm a Silicon Valley guy. I just think people from Silicon Valley can do anything."

73. "I tend to approach things from a physics framework. And physics teaches you to reason from first principles rather than by analogy."

74. "Tesla is here to stay and keep fighting for the electric car revolution."

75. "To make an embarrassing admission, I like video games. That's what got me into software engineering when I was a kid. I wanted to make money so I could buy a better computer to play better video games – nothing like saving the world."

76. "Biofuels such as ethanol require enormous amounts of cropland and end up displacing either food crops or natural wilderness, neither of which is good."

77. "Trying to read our DNA is like trying to understand software code with 90% of the code riddled with errors. It's very difficult in that case to understand and predict what that software code is going to do."

78. "In order to have your voice heard in Washington, you have to make some little contribution."

79. "FOR ALL THE SUPPORTERS OF TESLA OVER THE YEARS, AND IT'S BEEN SEVERAL YEARS NOW, AND THERE HAVE BEEN SOME VERY TOUGH TIMES, I'D JUST LIKE TO SAY, THANK YOU VERY MUCH. I DEEPLY APPRECIATE THE SUPPORT, PARTICULARLY THROUGH THE DARKEST TIMES."

80. I SAY SOMETHING AND THEN IT USUALLY HAPPENS. MAYBE NOT ON SCHEDULE, BUT IT USUALLY HAPPENS."

81. "I THINK WE ARE AT THE DAWN OF A NEW ERA IN COMMERCIAL SPACE EXPLORATION."

82. "IF YOU THINK BACK TO THE BEGINNING OF CELL PHONES, LAPTOPS OR REALLY ANY NEW TECHNOLOGY, IT'S ALWAYS EXPENSIVE."

83. "THE REASON WE SHOULD DO A CARBON TAX IS BECAUSE IT'S THE RIGHT THING TO DO. IT'S ECONOMICS 101 – ELEMENTARY STUFF."

84. "There are some important differences between me and Tony Stark; like, I have five kids, so I spend more time going to Disneyland than at parties."

85. "My opinion is it's a bridge too far to go to fully autonomous cars."

86. My vision is for a fully reusable rocket transport system between Earth and Mars that is able to re-fuel on Mars – this is very important – so you don't have to carry the return fuel when you go there."

87. "I don't think it's a good idea to plan to sell a company."

88. "I'm glad to see that BMW is bringing an electric car to market. That's cool."

89. "People should pursue what they're passionate about. That will make them happier than pretty much anything else."

90. "If humanity doesn't land on Mars in my lifetime, I would be very disappointed."

91. "It is theoretically possible to warp space-time itself, so you're not actually moving faster than the speed of light, but it's actually space that's moving."

92. "I would like to fly in space. Absolutely. That would be cool. I used to just do personally risky things, but now I've got kids and responsibilities, so I can't be my own test pilot. That wouldn't be a good idea. But I definitely want to fly as soon as it's a sensible thing to do."

93. "It's obviously tricky to convert cellulose to a useful biofuel. I think actually the most efficient way to use cellulose is to burn it in a co-generation power plant. That will yield the most energy and that's something you can do now."

94. "There's nothing… I've bought everything I want. I don't like yachts or anything; you know, I'm not a yacht person, and I've got pretty much the nicest plane I'd want to have."

95. "I always invest my own money in the companies that I create. I don't believe in the whole thing of just using other people's money. I don't think that's right. I'm not going to ask other people to invest in something if I'm not prepared to do it myself."

96. "I think most of the important stuff on the Internet has been built. There will be continued innovation, for sure, but the great problems of the Internet have essentially been solved."

97. "I'm actually wondering about putting in a roller coaster. You'd get in, and it would take you around the factory. Who else has a roller coaster?

98. "I think the high-tech industry is used to developing new things very quickly. It's the Silicon Valley way of doing business: you either move very quickly and you work hard to improve your product technology, or you get destroyed by some other company."

99. "The revolutionary breakthrough will come with rockets that are fully and rapidly reusable. We will never conquer Mars unless we do that. It'll be too expensive. The American colonies would never have been pioneered if the ships that crossed the ocean hadn't been reusable."

100. "There are really two things that have to occur in order for a new technology to be affordable to the mass market. One is you need economies of scale. The other is you need to iterate on the design. You need to go through a few versions."

101. "With DNA, you have to be able to tell which genes are turned on or off. Current DNA sequencing cannot do that. The next generation of DNA sequencing needs to be able to do this. If somebody invents this, then we can start to very precisely identify cures for diseases."

102. "I like the word 'autopilot' more than I like 'self-driving.' 'Self-driving' sounds like it's going to do something you don't want it to do. 'Autopilot' is a good thing to have in planes, and we should have it in cars."

103. "The finish line is usually a lot further away than you think."

104. "Boeing just took $20 billion and 10 years to improve the efficiency of their planes by 10 percent. That's pretty lame. I have a design in mind for a vertical liftoff supersonic jet that would be a really big improvement."

105. "It's not as though we can keep burning coal in our power plants. Coal is a finite resource too. We must find alternatives, and it's a better idea to find alternatives sooner than wait until we run out of coal, and in the meantime, put God knows how many trillions of tons of CO_2 that used to be buried under the ground into the atmosphere."

106. "It's important that we attempt to extend life beyond Earth now. It is the first time in the four billion-year history of Earth that it's been possible, and that window could be open for a long time – hopefully it is – or it could be open for a short time. We should err on the side of caution and do something now."

107. "If we're going to have any chance of sending stuff to other star systems, we need to be laser-focused on becoming a multi-planet civilization.

108. "SpaceX has the potential of saving the U.S. government $1 billion a year. We are opposed to creating an entrenched monopoly with no realistic means for anyone to compete."

109. "Even if producing CO2 was good for the environment, given that we're going to run out of hydrocarbons, we need to find some sustainable means of operating."

110. "If anyone has a vested interest in space solar power, it's me."

111. "I think long term you can see Tesla establishing factories in Europe, in other parts of the U.S. and in Asia."

112. "Tesla is becoming a real car company."

113. "I'd like to dial it back five or ten percent and try to have a vacation that's not just e-mail with a view.

114. "I think we have a duty to maintain the light of consciousness; to make sure it continues into the future."

115. "I'm personally a moderate and a registered independent, so I'm not strongly Democrat or strongly Republican."

116. "Selling an electric sports car creates an opportunity to fundamentally change the way America drives."

117. "Obviously Tesla is about helping solve the consumption of energy in a sustainable manner, but you need to production of energy in a sustainable manner."

118. "There's just no way around Newton's third law."

119. "Winning 'Motor Trend Car of the Year' is probably the closest thing to winning the Oscar or Emmy of the car industry."

120. "I think there are more politicians in favor of electric cars than against. There are still some that are against, and I think the reasoning for that varies depending on the person, but in some cases, they just don't believe in climate change – they think oil will last forever."

121. "I think Tesla will most likely develop its own autopilot system for the car, as I think it should be camera-based, no Lidar-based. However it is also possible we do something jointly with Google."

122. "From an evolutionary standpoint, human consciousness has not been around very long. A little light just went on after four and a half billion years. How often does that happen? Maybe it's quite rare."

123. "I try to construct a world that maximizes the probability that SpaceX continues its mission without me."

124. "If we could do high-speed rail in California just half a notch above what they've done on the Shanghai line in China, and if we had a straight path from L.A. to San Francisco, as well as the milk run, at least that would be progress."

125. I'm interested in things that change the world or that affect the future and wondrous, new technology where you see it and you're like, 'Wow, how did that even happen? How is that possible?'"

126. "You have to put in 80 hour, 80 to 100 hours a week, every week. If someone else is putting in 40 hours a week, you can achieve in four months, what it takes them a year to achieve."

127. When I was in university, I thought about what kind of problems were likely to affect the future of the world – the future of humanity."

128. "A GOOD FRAMEWORK FOR THINKING IS PHYSICS."

129. "I'M CONFIDENT THAT SOLAR WILL BEAT EVERYTHING – INCLUDING NATURAL GAS. IT MUST ACTUALLY. IF IT DOESN'T, WE'RE IN DEEP TROUBLE."

130. "THEY GO MY BEST FUCKING FRIEND TO LURE ME OUT OF HIDING SO THEY COULD BEAT ME UP. AND THAT FUCKING HURT. FOR SOME REASON, THEY DECIDED THAT I WAS IT, AND THEY WERE GOING TO GO AFTER ME NONSTOP. THAT'S WHAT MADE GROWING UP DIFFICULT. FOR A NUMBER OF YEARS THERE WAS NO RESPITE. YOU GET CHASED AROUND BY GANGS AT SCHOOL WHO TRIED TO BEAT THE SHIT OUT OF ME, AND THEN I'D COME HOME, AND IT WOULD JUST BE AWFUL THERE AS WELL."

131. "ARE THE EFFORTS RESULTING IN A BETTER PRODUCT OR SERVICE? IF THEY'RE NOT, STOP THOSE EFFORTS."

132. "WE'RE DOING THESE THINGS THAT SEEM UNLIKELY TO SUCCEED."

133. "All a company is, is a group of people that have gathered together to create a product or service. And so, depending on how talented and hardworking that group is, and degree to which they're focused, cohesively in a good direction, that will determine the success of the company. So do everything you can to gather great people, if you're creating a company."

134. "A lot of companies get confused; they spend money on things that don't actually make the product better. For example, at Tesla, we've never spent any money on advertising. We put all the money into R&D and manufacturing and design to try and make the car as good as possible."

135. "You're always going to buy the trusted brand, unless there's a big difference."

136. "WE ARE RUNNING THE MOST DANGEROUS EXPERIMENT IN HISTORY RIGHT NOW, WHICH IS TO SEE HOW MUCH CARBON DIOXIDE THE ATMOSPHERE CAN HANDLE BEFORE THERE IS AN ENVIRONMENTAL CATASTROPHE."

137. "USUALLY YOUR FRIENDS KNOW WHAT IS WRONG. BUT THEY DON'T WANT TO TELL YOU, BECAUSE THEY DON'T WANT TO HURT YOU."

138. "WHEN I WAS A KID, I WAS REALLY SCARED OF THE DARK. BUT THEN I SORT OF CAME TO UNDERSTAND 'OKAY, DARK REALLY MEANS THE ABSENCE OF PHOTONS IN THE VISIBLE WAVELENGTH. I THOUGHT IT WAS REALLY SILLY TO BE AFRAID OF A LACK OF PHOTONS. AND THEN I WASN'T AFRAID OF THE DARK ANYMORE."

139. "AN OBSESSIVE NATURE ABOUT THE QUALITY OF THE PRODUCT IS VERY IMPORTANT. SO, YOU KNOW, BEING OBSESSIVE COMPULSIVE IS A GOOD THING, IN THIS CONTEXT."

140. "Do something bold. You won't regret it."

141. "If you like what you're doing, you think about it even when you're not working. It's something that your mind is drawn to. And if you don't like it, you just really can't make it work, I think."

142. "If any entities are listening, please bless this launch."

~

More Titles in *The Little Black Book* series:

Alaska Noon
Albert Einstein
Benjamin Franklin
Bill Gates
Bruce Lee
Buddha
Ida B. Wells
Jesus Christ
Johnny Depp
Jon Stewart
Mahatma Gandhi
Mark Zuckerberg
Martin Luther King Jr.
Nicholas Cage
Nikola Tesla
Oprah Winfrey
Richard Branson
Russell Brand
Steve Jobs
Steven Colbert
Walt Disney

If there is someone you'd like to see added to *The Little Black Book* series, please leave a comment in this books review section on Amazon.com.

Made in the USA
Lexington, KY
14 September 2018